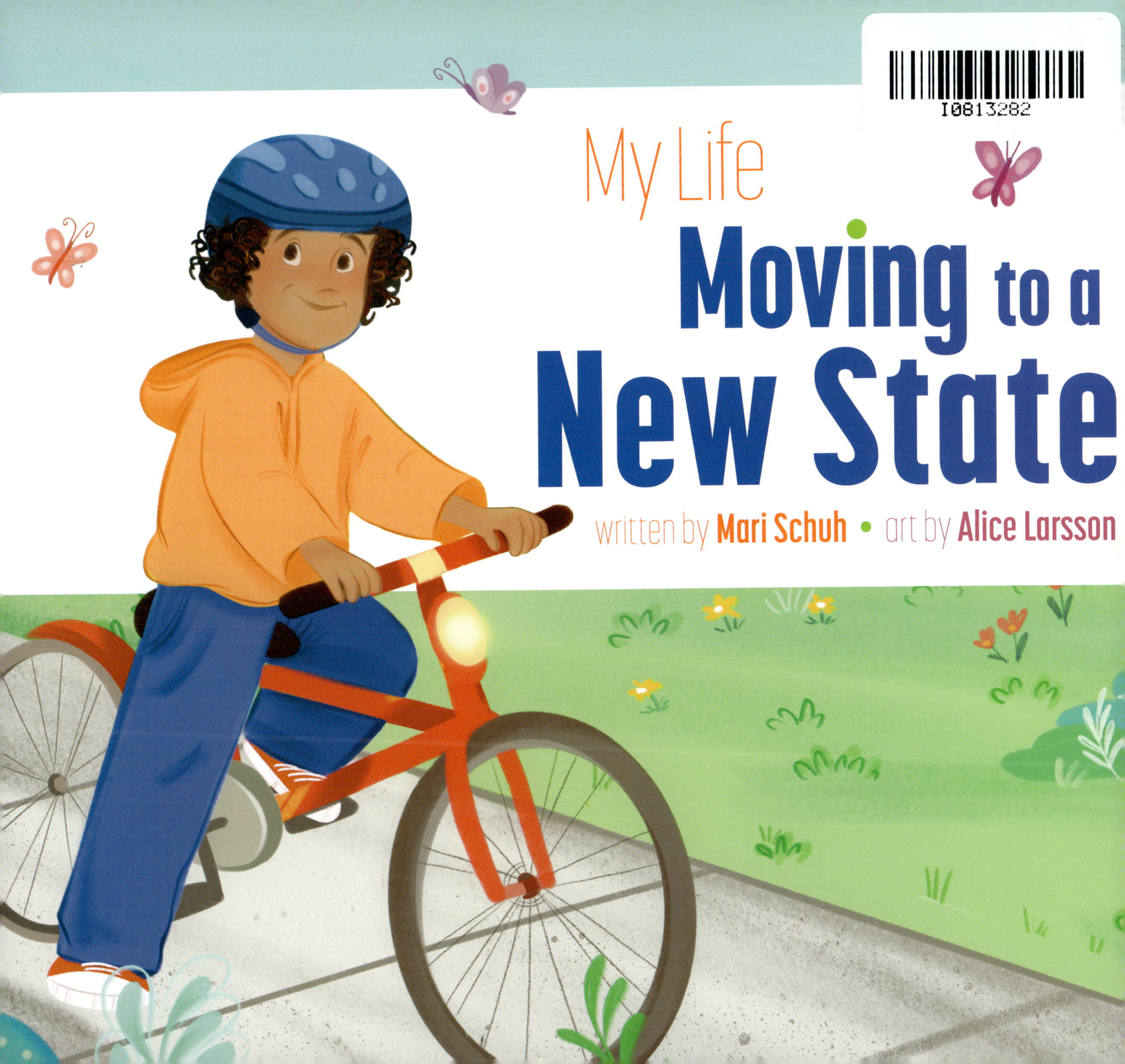

My Life

Moving to a New State

written by Mari Schuh • art by Alice Larsson

AMICUS ILLUSTRATED
is published by Amicus Learning, an imprint of Amicus
P.O. Box 227, Mankato, MN 56002
www.amicuspublishing.us

Editor: Rebecca Glaser
Series Designer: Kathleen Petelinsek
Book Designer: Emily Dietz

Library of Congress Cataloging-in-Publication Data
Names: Schuh, Mari C., 1975- author | Larsson, Alice illustrator
Title: My life moving to a new state / by Mari Schuh ; illustrated by Alice Larsson.
Description: Mankato, MN : Amicus Illustrated, 2026. | Series: My life with... | Includes bibliographical references. | Audience: Ages 6–9 | Audience: Grades 2–3 | Summary: "Tristan's life changes when he moves from Alabama to Iowa with his mom. Adjusting to a new state is challenging, but he finds joy in making new friends and exploring his neighborhood. Includes tips for respecting kids who have moved and a glossary."— Provided by publisher.
Identifiers: LCCN 2025014228 (print) | LCCN 2025014229 (ebook) | ISBN 9798892008860 library binding | ISBN 9798892009522 paperback | ISBN 9798896850182 ebook
Subjects: LCSH: Moving, Household—Juvenile literature | Change (Psychology)—Juvenile literature | LCGFT: Picture books
Classification: LCC TX307 S39 2026 (print) | LCC TX307 (ebook) | DDC 648/.9—dc23/eng/20250716
LC record available at https://lccn.loc.gov/2025014228
LC ebook record available at https://lccn.loc.gov/2025014229

Printed in China

About the Author
Mari Schuh's love of reading began with cereal boxes at the kitchen table. Today she is the author of hundreds of nonfiction books for beginning readers. With each book, Mari hopes she's helping kids learn a little bit more about the world around them. Find out more about her at marischuh.com.

About the Illustrator
Alice Larsson is a London-based illustrator originally from Sweden. A natural creative, she is thrilled to be able to connect characters and stories through her work. Outside of drawing, Alice loves spending time with family and friends, as well as reading books and traveling, which sparks her creativity.

Hi! My name is Tristan. I like to ride my bike and play video games. My mom and I moved to a new state. Let me tell you about what it's like to move across the country.

I grew up in Georgia and Alabama. I lived with my mom and dad. My friends and I liked to go to the trampoline park.

When I was 12 years old, my mom and dad got divorced. Many months later, my mom got a boyfriend. He lives in Iowa. Mom knew him a long time ago. She was friends with him before I was born.

We really liked living in Alabama. But sometimes my mom was lonely. She missed her boyfriend. We moved to Iowa so we could live near him.

My mom got a new job at a hospital in Iowa. Then we got ready to move. Mom started to pack, and I helped her. We were excited to start a new life in Iowa!

Moving can be exciting. But it is also stressful. I knew I would miss playing with my friends. It was hard to say goodbye. I felt so many emotions.

I also knew that I would miss my dad, so we made a plan to talk every day.

We traveled to Iowa in my mom's car. It took more than 15 hours! Our dog slept most of the trip. When we got tired, we stopped to take a break.

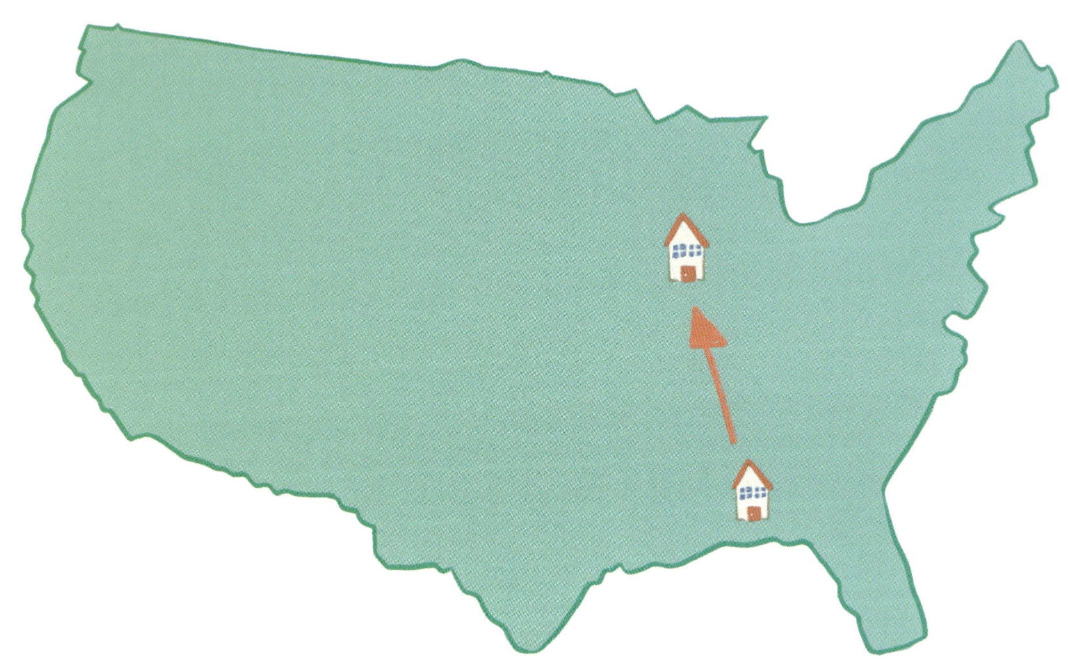

We like our new home in Iowa. Unpacking was easy. We didn't bring lots of stuff with us. We bought new things when we got to Iowa.

Our dog likes Iowa, too! We have a bigger yard. He has more space to run and play.

In Alabama, our neighborhood did not have sidewalks. I rode my bike on the street. Our new neighborhood has sidewalks. It's safer, so I ride my bike more often.

At my new school, it was easy to make new friends. We play together after school. Everyone is very nice to me.

I talk to my dad every day. And I often talk with my friends in Alabama.

On the weekends, we explore our new state with Mom's boyfriend. He has great ideas for fun things to do.

Neighbors often invite us over for cookouts. It helps me feel like a part of our new community.

I like living in Iowa. School is a bit harder here. But I enjoy it. When school is out for the summer, we'll visit Alabama. It will be fun to see my dad and my friends!

Meet Tristan

Hello! I'm Tristan. I live in Iowa with my mom. We have a dog named Yoshi. I enjoy riding my bike and going on hikes. Yoshi hikes with us, too! I like to eat fish, pizza, french fries, and chicken tenders. I also like to learn how things such as toilets work. When I grow up, I want to be a plumber.

Respecting Kids Who Have Moved to a New Place

Invite new students to play with you. You could make a new friend!

Be helpful to families that have just moved. Share ideas for restaurants they might like. Let them know where kids can play sports and join activities.

Families who have moved often live far away from grandparents and other relatives. Offer to help them if they need support.

Listen to a new friend's stories about their old community and share stories about your community. What can you learn from each other?

Moving can be hard. It can cause some kids to feel anxiety or fear. Being a kind person is helpful.

Don't bully new kids at school. Treat them how you would like to be treated.

Helpful Terms

cookout A fun gathering where food is cooked and eaten outdoors.

divorce The ending of a marriage by a court.

emotion A strong feeling such as love, sadness, fear, and happiness.

explore To travel through a new area to learn and have fun.

neighborhood A small area in a town or city where people live close to one another.

neighbors People who live in the same area.

Read More

Biermann, Renee. ***Facing Your Fear of Going to a New School.*** North Mankato, Minn.: Pebble Emerge, Capstone Imprint, 2023.

Cipriano, Jeri. ***Getting Ready to Move.*** Egremont, Mass.: Red Chair Press, 2021.

Gaertner, Meg. ***Moving.*** Mankato, Minn.: Little Blue House, 2022.

Websites

BEKINS: MOVING IS A BIG HOP!

https://www.bekins.com/wp-content/uploads/2023/07/BekinsColoringBookPDF_ToUse-1.pdf

Visit this website to download a coloring book about moving.

FANTASTIC FUN AND LEARNING: MOVING TO A NEW HOUSE

https://www.fantasticfunandlearning.com/wp-content/uploads/2014/07/Moving-to-a-New-House-Free-Printable-Book.pdf

Print this booklet. Then write your thoughts about your old home and your new home.

KIDMUNICATE: PREPARING TO MOVE TO A NEW HOUSE

https://kidmunicate.com/wp-content/uploads/2019/08/Social_Stories_Moving.pdf

Read a story about all the steps people go through when they move.

Every effort has been made to ensure that these websites are appropriate for children. However, because of the nature of the Internet, it is impossible to guarantee that these sites will remain active indefinitely or that their contents will not be altered.